# BIG
# ENGLISH 2

Mario Herrera • Christopher Sol Cruz

**PUPIL'S BOOK**

# Contents

| CLIL | Values | Phonics | I can... |
|------|--------|---------|----------|
| **Maths: Sums**<br>numbers 11–100<br>plus, minus, equals<br>10 minus 6 equals __<br>5 plus 5 equals __<br>**Project:** Maths poster | **Take turns.**<br>May I use the computer now?<br>Yes! Let's take turns. | **th**<br>that, the, then, this<br>bath, both, Maths,<br>mouth, thin, think, with | ...talk about what people are doing in the classroom.<br>...count to 100.<br>...talk about taking turns. |
| **Science: Muscles and bones**<br>bones, feet, hands, jump, kick, muscles, throw<br>We throw with our hands.<br>When we jump, we use (number) muscles.<br>**Project:** Body poster | **Play safely.**<br>safe, seesaw, skateboard, slide, swing<br>I want to play on the slide.<br>Always slide with your feet in front of you. | **ng, nk**<br>bang, king, ring, sing, wing<br>bank, ink, pink, sink, thank | ...say what people like doing.<br>...talk about how my body works.<br>...talk about playing safely. |
| **Social Science: Old and new things**<br>new, old<br>This is an old phone. / This phone is old.<br>These are new skates. / These skates are new.<br>**Project:** New and Old poster | **Be tidy.**<br>sink, toy box, washing machine | **oo**<br>boot, cool, food, moon, room, zoo<br>book, cook, foot, good, look | ...say where things are.<br>...talk about possessions.<br>...talk about new and old objects. |
| **Geography: Transport around the world**<br>bike, boat, bus, train<br>In Bangkok, many students go to school by boat.<br>**Project:** Go to School bar chart | **Cross the road safely.**<br>first, left, pedestrian crossing, right, road, wait | **ai, oa**<br>nail, rain, tail, train, wait<br>boat, coat, oak, road, soap | ...say what I want.<br>...describe where places are in town.<br>...talk about different kinds of transport. |
| **Social Science: Jobs around the world**<br>farmer, nurse, lifeguard, park ranger<br>grows food, helps ill people, helps people in the water, protects animals<br>A nurse helps ill people.<br>**Project:** I Want to Be flipbook | **Study hard and set goals.**<br>Art, Maths, Music, Science | **ar, er, or**<br>arm, art, car, cart<br>letter, singer, teacher<br>born, corn, for | ...talk about jobs.<br>...say what I want to be.<br>...talk about studying hard and setting goals. |
| **History: Old clocks**<br>hourglass, sand, shadow, sundial, water clock<br>We use clocks to tell time. A water clock uses water to tell time.<br>**Project:** Clock poster | **Be on time.**<br>I get my backpack ready the night before school.<br>I get up early on school days.<br>I get dressed quickly and eat breakfast.<br>I always get to school on time. | **ch, tch, sh**<br>chin, chop, lunch, rich<br>match, watch, witch<br>dish, fish, ship, shop | ...talk about times and daily activities.<br>...say when people do things.<br>...talk about different ways of telling time. |
| **Science: Where fruit comes from**<br>avocado, kiwi, pineapple, watermelon<br>healthy, unhealthy<br>Avocados come from Mexico.<br>**Project:** Where Fruit Comes From poster | **Choose healthy foods.**<br>apple, biscuit, carrots, crisps<br>No crisps for me, thanks.<br>Just one biscuit, please. | **ee, ie**<br>bee, cheese, feet, see, sheep<br>cried, flies, lie, pie, tie | ...talk about food I like.<br>...talk about healthy and unhealthy food.<br>...say where fruit comes from. |
| **Science: Animal habitats**<br>desert, forest, jungle, ocean<br>deer, fox, lizard, raccoon, seal, shark, tiger, whale<br>Lizards live in deserts.<br>**Project:** Animal Habitats poster | **Appreciate animals.**<br>amazing, beautiful, clever, strong | **ou, ow**<br>group, route, soup, toucan, you<br>clown, cow, down, owl, town | ...talk about what animals can do.<br>...talk about where animals live.<br>...talk about appreciating animals. |
| **Geography: Seasonal holidays**<br>spring, summer, autumn, winter<br>In England, people celebrate May Day. May Day is in spring.<br>**Project:** Festivals poster | **Be active all year.**<br>rake leaves, ride bikes, skate on ice, swim | **Alphabet** | ...name the months of the year.<br>...talk about what I do each month.<br>...talk about seasonal holidays. |

# unit 1
# In My Classroom

1:02
**1** Listen, look and say.

**1 colouring**

**2 counting**

**3 cutting**

**4 gluing**

**5 listening**

**6 watching a DVD**

**7 using the computer**

**8 writing**

**9 playing a game**

1:03
**2** Listen, find and say. **3** Play a game.

**4** **Listen and sing. Then look at 1 and find.**

## Here's My Classroom!

Look! Here's my classroom.
And here are my friends!
Peter, Sarah and Timothy,
Penny, Jack and Jen!

Peter is cutting paper.
Penny is writing her name.
Sarah is listening to a story
And Jack is playing a game.

Timothy is counting.
Jen is gluing.
We have fun and learn a lot.
What are your friends doing?

 **5** **Listen and find in 1. Then say.**

**6** **Look at 1. Ask and answer.**

What's she doing?

She's colouring.

**THINK BIG** What can we write?
What can we count?

1:09

**7** **Listen and read. How many Marias are there?**

**What's Maria Doing?**

What's Maria doing?

She's cutting paper.

1

No, she isn't. She's using the computer.

2

No, she isn't. Look!

Now Maria is writing on the board.

Maria

3

No! Look over here. Maria is gluing a picture.

4

**8** **Look at the story. Then match.**

1 She's cutting paper.

2 She's gluing pictures.

3 She's using the computer.

4 She's writing on the board.

a

b

**THINK BIG** **Are there any girls called Maria in your class? How many?**
**How many children are there with the same name? What are the names?**

**9** Listen. Help Jamie and Jenny make sentences.

1:10

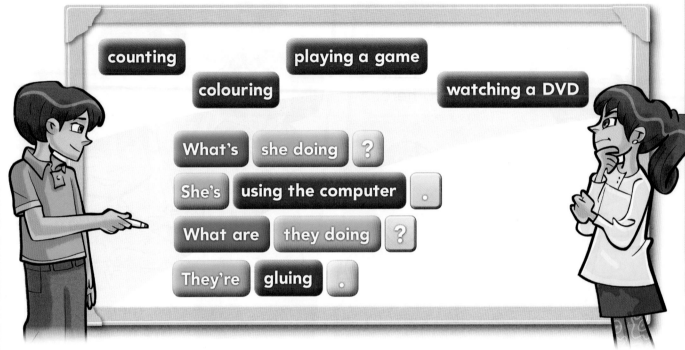

counting    playing a game

colouring    watching a DVD

What's | she doing | ?

She's | using the computer | .

What are | they doing | ?

They're | gluing | .

**10** Look and write.

**1** What's he _____? 
He's _____ his name.

**2** What's she _____? 
_____ a picture.

**3** _____ they _____? 
_____ to a story.

**4** _____? 
_____ paper.

1:12

 **Listen and stick. Then say.**

12 **Look at 11. Ask and answer. Use How many.**

How many computers are there?

There are two computers.

13 **Draw and write. Use There's or There are.**

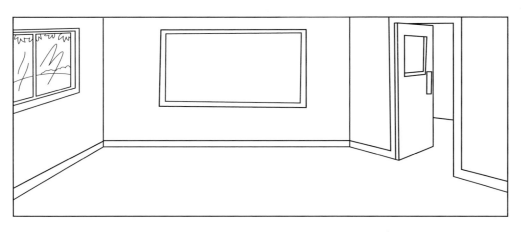

_____

_____

**Look, listen and repeat.**

| **11** eleven | **12** twelve | **13** thirteen | **14** fourteen | **15** fifteen | **16** sixteen |
| --- | --- | --- | --- | --- | --- |
| **17** seventeen | **18** eighteen | **19** nineteen | **20** twenty | **30** thirty | **40** forty |
| **50** fifty | **60** sixty | **70** seventy | **80** eighty | **90** ninety | **100** one hundred |

 **Look, listen and circle + or –. Then answer.**

| + | – | = |
| --- | --- | --- |
| plus | minus | equals |

**1**

    10    + / –    5    = _____ footballs

**2**

    16    + / –    3    = _____ pencils

**3**

    20    + / –    20    = _____ fingers

 **THINK BIG** How many children are there in your class? How old is your grandma or grandad?

**1:15**

**16  Listen and circle.**

1  **17 / 70**      2  **59 / 95**
3  **89 / 69**      4  **31 / 33**
5  **47 / 27**      6  **23 / 22**

 **1:16**

**17  Count and write. Then listen and check.**

1  $3 + 7 =$ ☐       2  $14 + 6 =$ ☐

3  $30 + 30 =$ ☐     4  $70 + 5 =$ ☐

5  $8 - 2 =$ ☐       6  $18 - 4 =$ ☐

7  $60 - 10 =$ ☐     8  $40 - 5 =$ ☐

## PROJECT

**18  Make a Maths poster. Then present it to the class.**

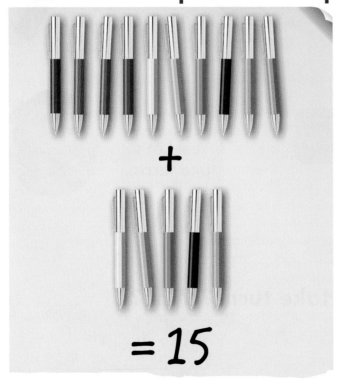

$+$

$= 15$

Ten pens plus five pens equals fifteen pens.

**Listen and look. Number in order.**

a

b

c

☐ ☐ ☐

**20** **Take turns. Ask and answer. Do the actions.**

May I use the computer now?

Yes! Let's take turns.

**THINK BIG** **Is it good to take turns? Why?**

**21** **Listen, look and repeat.** `1:18`

**1** th          **2** th

**22** **Listen and find. Then say.** `1:19`

**bath**

**thin**

**this**

**that**

**23** **Listen and blend the sounds.** `1:20`

**1** th-e        the          **2** th-e-n      then

**3** b-o-th    both          **4** w-i-th       with

**5** p-a-th    path          **6** M-a-th-s  Maths

**24** **Underline th and th. Then listen and chant.** `1:21`

There are three crocodiles
In the bath.
They've got thin mouths
But big teeth!
Look out! Look out!

**25** Listen and find. Say Picture 1 or Picture 2. Then ask and answer.

**Picture 1**

**Picture 2**

In Picture 1, what are they doing?

In Picture 1, they're playing a game.

**26** **Look and write.**

**1** _____
shapes.

**2** _____
her name.

**3** _____
to a story.

**4** _____
a DVD.

**5** _____
a picture.

**6** _____
his fingers.

**27** **Count and write. Use There's or There are.**

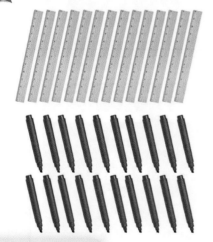

**1** _____

_____ rulers.

**2** _____

_____ rubber.

**3** _____

_____ marker pens.

**I Can**

☐ talk about what people are doing in the classroom.

☐ count to 100.

☐ talk about taking turns.

# unit 2 My Games

**1:24**

**1 Listen, look and say.**

1 flying kites

2 playing volleyball

3 playing tennis

4 climbing trees

7 skateboarding

5 doing gymnastics

6 ice skating

8 riding my bike

**1:25**

**2 Listen, find and say.**    **3 Play a game.**

**16** Unit 2 vocabulary (outdoor activities)

**5** **Listen and sing. Then look at 1 and find.**

## Come On and Play

We're playing in the playground.
There are a lot of games to play.
Football, tennis and volleyball.
What do you want to play today?

Paul likes playing on the swings.
Emma likes running and climbing.
We all love riding our bikes.
Tell us! What do you like doing?

We're playing in the playground.
It's always so much fun.
Come on and play with us.
We play with everyone!

1:28
**5** **Listen and ✔.**

a 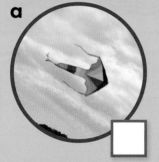 ☐

b  ☐

c  ☐

d  ☐

**6** **Look at 1. Ask and answer.**

 I like playing volleyball.

Number 2.

**THINK BIG** What games can children play in the playground?
What games can children play in the classroom?

1:30

**7** **Listen and read. What does Jenny like doing?**

We Like Playing Together!

This is a nice playground!

Yes, it is. What do you like doing in the playground?

1

I like playing football. My sister loves skateboarding.

2

What does your brother like doing?

He loves playing volleyball.

3

We like playing together, too.

How can you do that?

4

**8** **Look at the story. Then circle.**

 **1** likes **playing football / riding his bike**.

**2** loves **playing tennis / skateboarding**.

 **3** likes **playing volleyball / flying kites**.

**THINK BIG** **What do you like playing in the playground?**
**What team games do you know?**
**Do you like playing in a team? Why?**

**1:31**

**9** Listen. Help Jamie and Jenny make sentences.

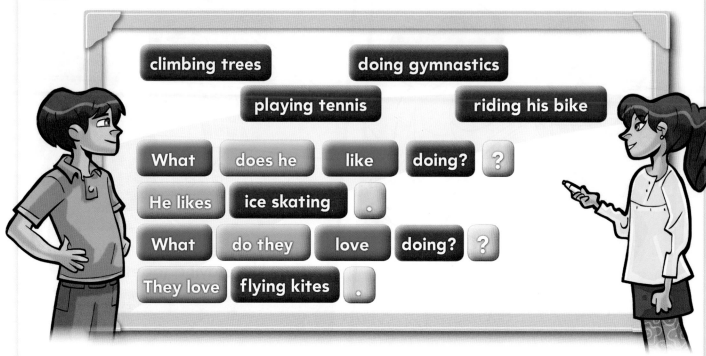

| climbing trees | | doing gymnastics |
|---|---|---|

| playing tennis | | riding his bike |
|---|---|---|

| What | does he | like | doing? | ? |

| He likes | ice skating | . |

| What | do they | love | doing? | ? |

| They love | flying kites | . |

**10** Look and write. Use **like** or **love**.

**1** What _____ she like doing?
She likes _____.

**2** What _____ they love _____?
They _____.

**3** _____ you _____?
I _____.

**4** _____ ?
_____.

## 11 Listen and stick. Then say.

1:33

## 12 Look at 11. Ask and answer.

 What do they love doing?

They love flying kites.

## 13 Write and draw.

I love _____

_____

_____

_____.

1:34

**14** **Look, listen and repeat.**

# 13   26   27   34   70

 1:35

**15** **Look, listen and read. Write the numbers from 14.**

Playing is fun. When we move, we use our bones and muscles. Bones and muscles help us play.

We throw with our hands. Our hands have got lots of bones. One hand has got ¹____ bones.

We kick with our feet. Our feet have got lots of bones, too. One foot has got ²____ bones. When we throw a ball, we use ³____ muscles. When we kick a ball, we use ⁴____ muscles.

When we jump, we use more than ⁵____ muscles.

Muscle →

Bone →

We need to take good care of our bones and muscles.

**THINK BIG** **What parts of our body do we climb trees with?**

**16 Read and circle.**

1 We throw with our **hands** / **feet**.
2 We kick with our **hands** / **feet**.
3 When we throw a ball, we use 34 **muscles** / **bones**.
4 When we kick a ball, we use **13** / **70** muscles.
5 One hand has got **26** / **27** bones.
6 One foot has got **34** / **26** bones.

**17 Play a game.**

climb    jump    kick    skip    throw

We throw with our feet.

False. We kick with our feet.

**PROJECT**

**18 Make a Body poster. Then present it to the class.**

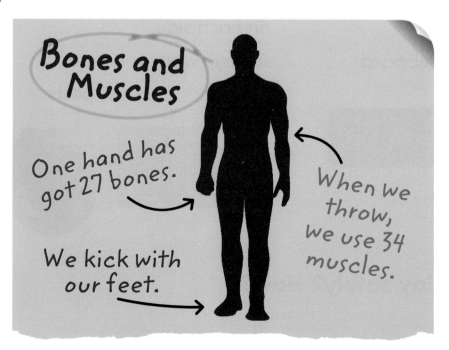

Bones and Muscles

One hand has got 27 bones.

When we throw, we use 34 muscles.

We kick with our feet.

We throw with our hands.

1:37

**19** **Listen and number.**

**a**

**b**

**c**

**d**

skateboard      swing      seesaw      slide

1:38

**20** **Listen and write. Then say.**

feet    hands    knee    leg

**A**

**1** I want to play on the slide.

**2** I want to play on the swing.

**3** I want to play on the seesaw.

**4** I want to skateboard.

**B**

Always slide with your _____ in front of you.

Always sit down and hold on with both _____.

Always put one _____ on each side.

Always wear a helmet and _____ pads.

> I want to play on the slide.

> Always slide with your feet in front of you.

**TH∎NK BIG** **Do you play safely? How?**

**21** 1:39 **Listen, look and repeat.**

**1** ng          **2** nk

 **22** 1:40 **Listen and find. Then say.**

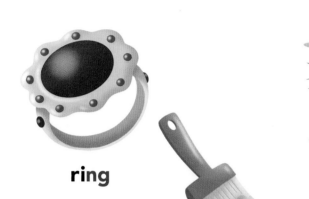

ring

pink

bang

ink

 **21** 1:41 **Listen and blend the sounds.**

**1** k-i-ng    king              **2** w-i-ng    wing

**3** th-a-nk   thank            **4** s-i-ng     sing

**5** b-a-nk    bank             **6** s-i-nk     sink

 **22** 1:42 **Underline ng and nk. Then listen and chant.**

Sing a song about a king.
Thank you! Thank you!
He's got a big, pink ring
And big, blue wings.
Thank you! Thank you!

**25** **Work in groups. Play the Memory game.**

**Pupil 1:**
What do you like doing in the playground? Say.

**Pupil 2:**
Talk about Pupil 1. What does she like doing? Then say and act out what you like doing.

> I like playing volleyball.

> Susan likes playing volleyball. I like riding my bike.

> Susan likes playing volleyball. Peter likes riding his bike. I like ice skating.

**Pupil 3:**
Talk about Pupils 1 and 2. Then say and act out what you like doing.

**Play with your group. Can you remember what everyone likes doing?**

**26** **Look and write. Use like or love.**

**1** _____

flying kites.

**2** _____

playing tennis.

**3** _____

playing football.

**4** _____

ice skating.

**27** **Answer the questions.**

**1** What do you like doing?

_____

**2** What do your friends love doing?

_____

**28** **Read and circle.**

**1** When we throw, we use our **feet** / **hands**.
**2** When we jump, we use our **arms** / **legs**.
**3** When we kick, we use our **feet** / **fingers**.
**4** When we dance, we use our **nose** / **toes**.

**I Can**

☐ say what people like doing.

☐ talk about how my body works.

☐ talk about playing safely.

# unit 3

# In My House

 **1** 1:44 **Listen, look and say.**

## living room

1 table
2 chair
3 sofa
4 DVD player
5 TV

## bathroom

6 bath

## kitchen

7 fridge
8 sink
9 cooker

## bedroom

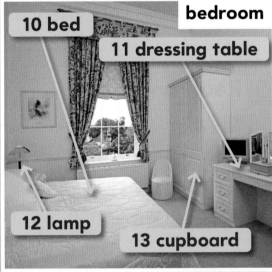

10 bed
11 dressing table
12 lamp
13 cupboard

 **2** 1:45 **Listen, find and say.** **3** **Play a game.**

**4** Listen and sing. Then look at 1 and find.

## Where Are My Keys?

Where are my keys, Mum?
Your keys are on the chair.
The chair? Which chair?
There are chairs everywhere!

There's a chair in the living room
And one in the bedroom, too.
There are chairs in the dining room.
I don't know which chair. Do you?

Your keys are where you left them.
Put on your glasses and see.
They're on the chair behind you.
My keys are there! Silly me!

**5** Listen and look at 1. Say yes or no.

**6** Look at 1. Ask and answer.

Where's the bath?

It's in the bathroom.

**THINK BIG** What rooms in a house do we use for washing?
What rooms in a house do we use for eating?

**1:50**

**7** Listen and read. How many cousins has Jamie got?

**A Family Visit**

Who are they, Jamie?

They're my aunt and uncle. My aunt is my mum's sister.

**1**

These are my cousins. They're my aunt and uncle's children.

**2**

Where are your cousins now?

They're in the kitchen. Look!

**3**

Where are they now?

They're in my bedroom. They're jumping on my bed!

**4**

> Jamie, where's the TV?
>
> It's in the living room.

**5**

> Great! They're watching TV. They're quiet!

**6**

**8** **Look and write.**

| bedroom | living room | kitchen |

**1** Jamie's cousins are in the _____.

**2** Now they're in Jamie's _____.

**3** The TV is in the _____.

**THINK BIG** My father's brother is my...
My father's sister is my...
My uncle's son is my...

1:51

**9** **Listen. Help Jamie and Jenny make sentences.**

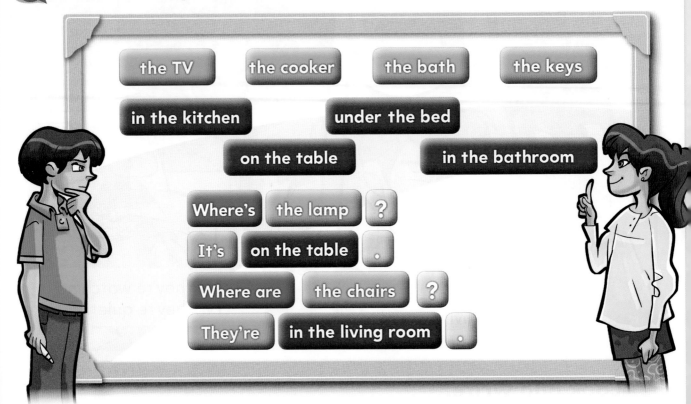

the TV    the cooker    the bath    the keys

in the kitchen    under the bed

on the table    in the bathroom

Where's | the lamp | ?

It's | on the table | .

Where are | the chairs | ?

They're | in the living room | .

**10** **Look and write. Use Where's or Where are.**

between     behind     in front of     next to

1 _____ the table?

It's _____ the TV and the sofa.

2 _____ the lamps?

They're _____ the sofa.

3 _____ the chair?

_____ the table.

4 _____ the TV?

_____ the table.

1:52

**11 Listen and stick. Then ask and answer.**

 Where are Ben's shoes?

Ben's shoes are in the kitchen.

**12 Write and draw. Where's your uncle's phone?**

My uncle's phone is

_____

_____.

language practice (*Where are Ben's shoes? Ben's shoes are in the kitchen.*) Unit 3   **33**

**1:53** **13** **Look, listen and repeat.**

**1 old**

**2 new**

 **1:54** **14** **Look, listen and read. What things are new?**

**1** These things are old.

This is an old bike.

This jacket is old.

These skates are old.

**2** These things are new.

This bike is new.

This is a new jacket.

These are new skates.

**THINK BIG** Find one old thing and one new thing in your classroom.
Name one old thing and one new thing in your home.

**15** **Write old or new. Match.**

**1**

**2**

**3**

**4**

**a**

**b**

**c**

**d**

**16** **Look at 15. Play the game.**

This phone is old.

These cars are new.

Number 1.

Number 3.

**PROJECT**

**17** **Make a New and Old poster. Then present it to the class.**

Old

Ye Olde Manuscript

New

This bike is new.
This car is old.

1:55

 **18** **Listen and write. Then say.**

sink     toy box
washing machine

**1** I put my toys in the _____.

**2** I put my dirty dishes in the _____.

**3** I put my dirty clothes in the

_____.

**19** **How do you keep your home tidy?
Act it out. Then guess.**

You put your clothes
in the cupboard.

**THINK
BIG** **Is it good to be tidy at home? Why?
Is it good to be tidy in class? Why?**

**1:57**
**20** **Listen, look and repeat.**

1 OO          2 OO

**1:58**
**21** **Listen and find. Then say.**

**moon**

b**oo**k

**zoo**

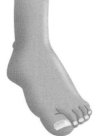

f**oo**t

**1:59**
**22** **Listen and blend the sounds.**

| | | | | |
|---|---|---|---|---|
| **1** r-oo-m | room | **2** l-oo-k | look |
| **3** f-oo-d | food | **4** c-oo-k | cook |
| **5** c-oo-l | cool | **6** g-oo-d | good |

**1:60**
**23** **Underline oo and oo. Then listen and chant.**

Look in my cook book.
The food is good!
The food is cool!

**24** Look and choose a room. Draw a line.

keys

phone

football

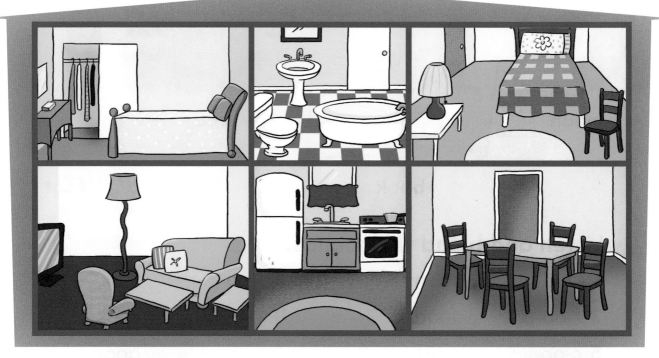

glasses

skates

hat

**25** Look at 24. Ask and answer.

Where are the keys?

They're on the table in front of the bed.

**26** **Look and write. Use old or new.**

baths
chairs
cooker
dressing table
fridge
lamp

**1** This _____ is _____.

**2** This _____ is _____.

**3** This is a _____ _____.

**4** This is a _____ _____.

**5** These _____ are _____.

**6** These are _____ _____.

**27** **Write.**

are   glasses   in   on   Tina's   where's

**James:** Kate, ¹_____ my Maths book?

**Kate:** It's ²_____ the dining room ³_____ the table.

**James:** Thanks. Hey, ⁴_____ those your ⁵_____?

**Kate:** No, they're ⁶_____ glasses.

**I Can**

☐ say where things are.
☐ talk about possessions.
☐ talk about new and old objects.

**Do I Know It?**

### 1 Think about it. Look and circle. Practise.

😊 I know this.   😕 I don't know this.

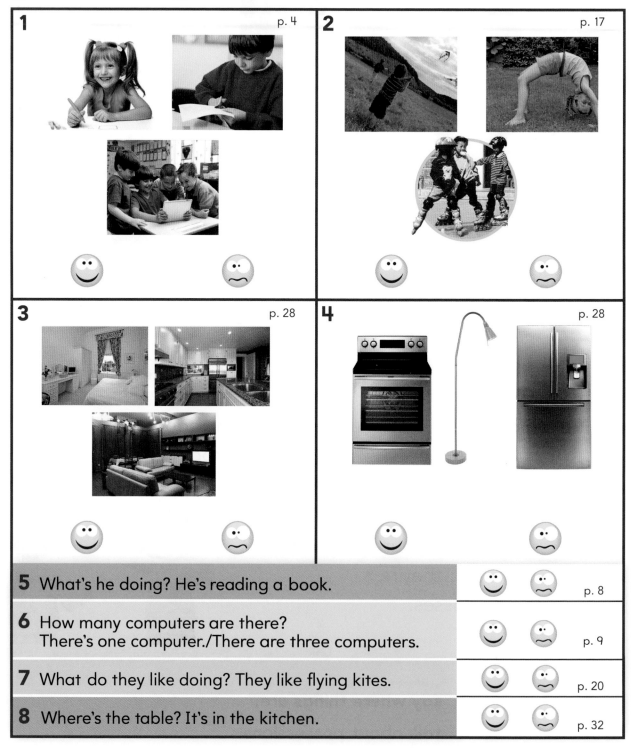

| | |
|---|---|
| **5** What's he doing? He's reading a book. | 😊 😕 p. 8 |
| **6** How many computers are there? There's one computer./There are three computers. | 😊 😕 p. 9 |
| **7** What do they like doing? They like flying kites. | 😊 😕 p. 20 |
| **8** Where's the table? It's in the kitchen. | 😊 😕 p. 32 |

1:62

**2 Get ready.**

**A** Look, listen and write.

> between    on    under

| | |
|---|---|
| **Miss Davis:** | What do you like doing in the playground? |
| **Adam:** | I like playing ¹_____ the swings. |
| **Beth:** | Katy and I like playing football. |
| **Katy:** | And I like skating! |
| **Miss Davis:** | OK. Where's the football? |
| **Beth:** | It's ²_____ the chair. |
| **Miss Davis:** | And where are Katy's skates? |
| **Adam:** | They're ³_____ the two chairs. |
| **Miss Davis:** | OK. Let's go outside! |

**B** Look at A and point. Ask and answer with a partner.

> What's she doing?          She's colouring a picture.

**C** Look at A. Point and say how many. Use There's or There are.

> chairs    football    teacher

1
2
3
4
5
6
7
8
9

**3** **Get set.**

 Cut out the cards on page 139.
Now you're ready to **Go!**

1:63

**4** **Go!**

**A** Look at the cards and write. Listen and check.

| are colouring on reading they're under |

**1** In pictures 1 and 2, they're _____ a picture.

**2** In pictures 3 and 4, _____ playing football.

**3** In pictures 1 and 3, they're _____ a book.

**4** In pictures 2 and 4, there's a basketball _____ the table.

**5** In pictures 1, 2, 3 and 4, there _____ keys _____ the table.

**B** Point to a card. Ask and answer with a partner.

What do they like doing?

They like playing football.

Where are the keys?

They're on the table.

**5** **Write or draw.**

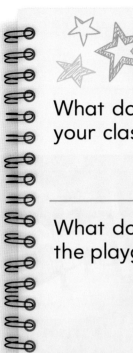

# All About Me

| | |
|---|---|
| What do you like doing in your classroom? | Where do you like reading? |
| What do you like doing in the playground? | Where are your toys? |

### Do I Know It Now?

**6** **Think about it.**

**A** Go to page 40. Look and circle again.

**B** Tick (✔).

☐ I can start the next unit.

☐ I can ask my teacher for help and then start the next unit.

☐ I can practise and then start the next unit.

**7** **Rate this Checkpoint. Colour the stars.**

easy     hard

fun     not fun

## 2:01

**1** Listen, look and say.

**1 cinema**

**2 petrol station**

**3 restaurant**

**4 train station**

**5 bus stop**

**6 post office**

**7 bookshop**

**8 computer shop**

**9 supermarket**

**10 shopping centre**

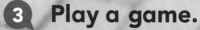

**11 bank**

## 2:02

**2** Listen, find and say.    **3** Play a game.

**4** **Listen and sing. Then look at 1 and find.**

## Maps Are Great!

Where's the bookshop?
I want to buy a book.
Here, I've got a map.
Come on. Let's take a look!

The bookshop is in River Street.
It isn't far from us.
Do you want to walk there?
No, thanks! Let's take the bus!

I want to send a letter, too.
Is there a post office?
Do you know?
I'm looking at the map.
Yes, there is.
It's near the bookshop.
Come on. Let's go.

Maps are really great.
I use them every day.
In town or out of town
They help me find my way!

 **5** **Listen and number.**

**6** **Look at 5. Ask and answer.**

Where's the restaurant?

It's in Castle Road. It's next to the petrol station.

**THINK BIG** **What can you see at a cinema?**
**What can you eat in a restaurant?**

**7** Listen and read. Where are Jenny and her dad?

2:07

# Is There a Bookshop?

Do you want to come to the shopping centre, Jenny?

Yes, OK.

I want to buy a book. Is there a bookshop?

Yes, there is. Look!

1

2

I want to buy a computer game. Is there a computer shop?

Yes, there is. It's here.

3

I'm hungry. Let's eat first.

OK. There are restaurants over there!

4

**8** **Look and read. Write.**

**1** Jenny's dad wants to buy a book at the _____.

**2** Jenny wants to buy a _____ _____ at the computer shop.

**3** Jenny and her dad want to eat lunch at a _____.

**4** Jenny wants pizza and _____.

**5** Dad hasn't got his _____.

**THINK BIG** Do you like shopping?
Where do you go shopping in?
What's your favourite shop?
What do you like buying?

2:08

**9** Listen. Help Jamie and Jenny make sentences.

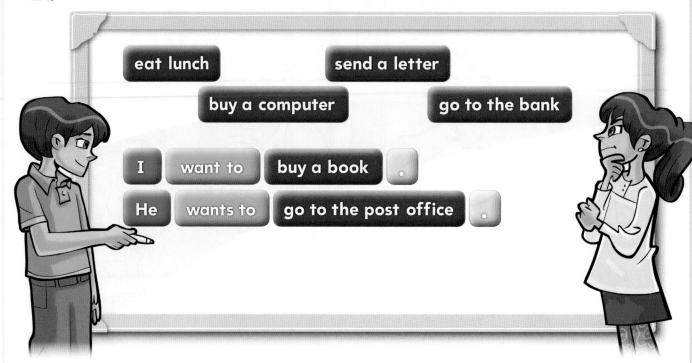

eat lunch    send a letter

buy a computer    go to the bank

I | want to | buy a book | .

He | wants to | go to the post office | .

**10** Write want to or wants to.

**1** Mum _____ buy bananas.

**2** I _____ buy a new jacket.

**3** My brother and I _____ eat sandwiches.

**4** Paula and Richard _____ watch a film.

**5** We _____ go to the bus stop.

**6** My cousin _____ buy a football.

**7** They _____ go to the bank.

**8** I _____ send a letter.

2:09

## 11 Listen and stick. Then say.

## 12 Look at 11. Ask and answer.

Is there a bank near here?

Yes, there is. It's in Cherry Street.

Is there a post office in Elm Road?

No, there isn't. It's in Park Street next to the park.

## 13 Write and draw. Where's the shopping centre?

The shopping centre is

_____

_____

_____.

2:10

**14** **Look, listen and repeat.**

**1 train**

**2 bike**

**3 bus**

**4 boat**

2:11

**15** **Listen and write. How do children go to school in these places?**

| Bangkok | Beijing | London | Mexico City |

**1** In _____, many children go to school by bike.

**2** In _____, many children go to school by boat.

**3** In _____, some children go to school by train.

**4** In _____, many children go to school by bus.

**THINK BIG** **What other ways can children go to school?**
**How do children go to school in your country?**

2:12

**16** **Listen and match.**

1   2   3   4

a   b   c   d

**17** **Look at 16. Do a class survey.**

|  | bus | train | boat | bike | other |
|---|---|---|---|---|---|
| Sam | ✔ | | | | |
| | | | | | |

Sam, how do you go to school?

I go to school by bus.

**PROJECT**

**18** **Make a Go to School bar chart. Then present it to the class.**

In my class, four children go to school by bus.

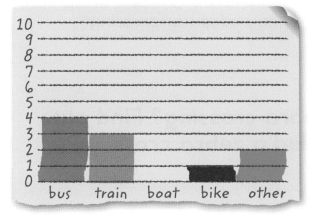

2:13

**19 Listen and write. Then say.**

cross  look  wait

**1** First, I always _____ at the pedestrian crossing.

**2** Second, I _____ for the green man.

**3** Last, I _____ left, then right, then left again before I cross the road.

**20 Look and number. Then ask and answer.**

a

b

c

How do you cross the road safely?

First, I always cross at the pedestrian crossing.

**THINK BIG** What is a zebra crossing? Find out. Why is it called a zebra crossing?

2:14

 **21** **Listen, look and repeat.**

**1** ai          **2** oa

2:15

**22** **Listen and find. Then say.**

**train**

**rain**

**boat**

**coat**

2:16

**23** **Listen and blend the sounds.**

**1** n-ai-l     nail          **2** oa-k     oak

**3** t-ai-l     tail          **4** s-oa-p   soap

**5** w-ai-t     wait          **6** r-oa-d   road

2:17

**24** **Underline ai and oa. Then listen and chant.**

Wear a coat
To sail the boat!
Drive the train
In the rain!

**25** **Work in two groups. Make sentence cards.**

**Group A:**
Write sentences starting with
*I want to.* Write a different
activity for each pupil in
the group.

**Group B:**
Write sentences starting with
*There's a.* Write a different
place for each pupil in
the group.

**26** **Groups A and B: Take turns to read your cards.
Find your match.**

I want to buy a book.

Yes, a match!

There's a bookshop
near here.

## 27 Read and match.

1 I want to buy a book.
2 Tim wants to see a film.
3 Mum and Dad want to put petrol in the car.
4 Ben wants to send a letter.

a There's a cinema near the bus stop.
b There's a post office in Main Street.
c There's a bookshop in Maple Road.
d There's a petrol station next to the bank.

## 28 Look and write. Use by.

1 Many children go to school

_____.

2 My sister comes home

_____.

3 My mum goes to the bank

_____.

## 29 Circle the correct answers.

**Maria:** Dad **want to / wants to** eat Chinese food for dinner. But I **want to / wants to** eat Mexican food.

**Mum:** **There is / Is there** a Chinese restaurant near here?

**Tom:** Yes, **there is / there isn't**. Let's go there.

 **I Can**

☐ say what I want.

☐ describe where places are in town.

☐ talk about different kinds of transport.

# unit 5

## My Dream Job

2:20

**1** Listen, look and say.

**1 actor**

**2 artist**

**3 dancer**

**4 doctor**

**5 writer**

**6 pilot**

**7 singer**

**8 athlete**

**9 teacher**

**10 chef**

**11 vet**

2:21

**2** Listen, find and say.

**3** Play a game.

# 4 Listen and chant. Then look at 1 and find.

## Hey, What Do You Want to Be?

Hey, what do you want to be?
You have to choose just one.
There are so many different jobs.
I want one that is fun!

I want to be a dancer
And an athlete, too.
Or maybe a teacher.
What about you?

I want to be an actor
And I want to be a vet.
I want to be a pilot, too.
Then I can fly a jet!

Chorus

# 5 Listen and write.

**1** I want to be a _____.   **2** I want to be a _____.   **3** I want to be a _____.

# 6 Look at 1. Ask and answer.

What do you want to be?

I want to be a chef.

**THINK BIG** What jobs do people do at school?
What jobs do people do in town?

2:26

**7** **Listen and read. What does Jamie like doing?**

1. What do you want to be, Jenny?

Dream Jobs!

I want to be a singer. I like singing.

2. What do you want to be, Dan?

I want to be a writer. I like writing stories.

3. What's your dream job, Maria?

I want to be a dancer. I like dancing.

4. Jamie, your sister wants to be a singer. What do you want to be?

I want to be a chef.

**8** **Look at the story. Write.**

**1** Jenny wants to be a _____.

**2** Dan wants to be a _____.

**3** Maria wants to be a _____.

**4** Jamie wants to be a _____.

**THINK BIG** **What's your favourite job in the story? Why?**
**What do you want to be? Why?**

**9** 2:27 **Listen. Help Jamie and Jenny make sentences.**

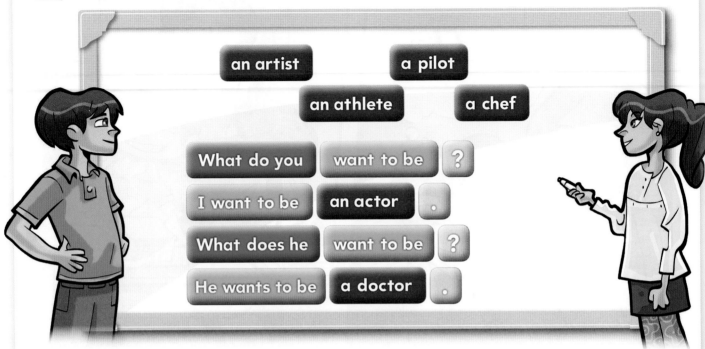

an artist    a pilot

an athlete    a chef

What do you    want to be    ?

I want to be    an actor    .

What does he    want to be    ?

He wants to be    a doctor    .

**10** **Look and write. Then draw and write.**

**1** What does she want to be?    **2** What does he want to be?

_____    _____

**3** What does Sally want to be?    **4** What do you want to be?

_____    _____

2:28

**11** **Listen and stick. Then say.**

1

2

3

4

**12** **Look at 11. Ask and answer.**

What does he want to be?

He wants to be a singer.

**13** **Write. Use do or does.**

**1** What _____ he want to be?

**2** What _____ they want to be?

**3** What _____ your cousins want to be?

**4** What _____ your brother/sister want to be?

2:29

**14** **Look, listen and repeat.**

**1 park ranger**     **2 lifeguard**     **3 farmer**     **4 nurse**

2:30

**15** **Look, listen and read. What does David want to be?**

1    I'm Karen. I live in Australia. I love swimming. I want to be a lifeguard. A lifeguard helps people in the water.

2    I'm Juma. I live in Botswana, in Africa. I like animals. I want to be a park ranger like my dad. A park ranger protects animals.

3    I'm David. I'm from England. I like riding on my dad's tractor. My dad's a farmer. I want to be a farmer, too. A farmer grows food.

4    I'm Maria. I'm from Spain. I like helping people. I want to be a nurse. A nurse helps ill people.

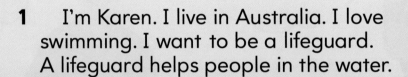
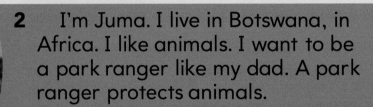
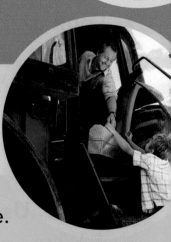

**THINK BIG** **Think of five more jobs that help people or animals.**

**16** **Circle T for true or F for false.**

1 David wants to be a farmer.      **T F**

2 Juma lives in Botswana, Africa.      **T F**

3 Karen wants to be a park ranger.      **T F**

4 A farmer grows food.      **T F**

5 A park ranger protects children.      **T F**

6 A nurse helps ill people.      **T F**

**17** **Look at 15 and play a game.**

Do you like swimming?    No.

Do you like riding a tractor?    Yes.

Do you want to be a farmer?    Yes.

**PROJECT**

**18** **Make an I Want to Be flipbook. Then present it to the class.**

I want to be a doctor. A doctor helps people.

1  2  3  4

2:32

**19** **Listen and write. Then say.**

| Art | Maths | Music | Science |

**1** I like _____.
I want to be a teacher.

**2** I like _____.
I want to be a doctor.

**3** I like _____.
I want to be a pilot.

**4** I like _____.
I want to be an artist.

**20** **Tell a partner what you want to be. Then act it out.**

I like Music. I want to be a singer.

I like Music, too. I want to be a dancer.

**THINK BIG** You like _____. What other jobs can you do?
**a** Art    **b** Music    **c** Maths    **d** Science

**2:33**

**21** **Listen, look and repeat.**

**1** ar          **2** er          **3** or

**2:34**

**22** **Listen and find. Then say.**

**arm**

**teacher**

**car**

**corn**

**2:35**

**23** **Listen and blend the sounds.**

**1** c-ar-t          cart          **2** s-i-ng-er          singer

**3** f-or          for          **4** ar-t          art

**5** b-or-n          born          **6** l-e-tt-er          letter

**2:36**

**24** **Underline ar, er and or. Then listen and chant.**

I want to be a singer
Or an artist painting art.
I want to be a teacher
Or a farmer with a cart!

**25** Work in small groups. Ask "What do you want to be?". Write names and jobs.

| Name | Wants to Be |
|------|-------------|
| Michael | a pilot |
|  |  |
|  |  |
|  |  |
|  |  |

**26** Count how many pupils in 25 want each job. Write a list.

| Job | How Many |
|-----|----------|
| Doctor | 3 |
|  |  |
|  |  |

**27** Look at this bar chart. Make a bar chart for your group and talk about it.

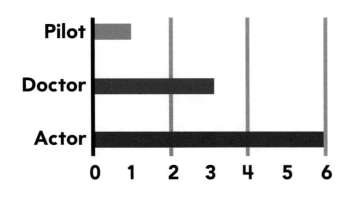

Pilot
Doctor
Actor
0  1  2  3  4  5  6

One pupil wants to be a pilot. Three pupils want to be doctors.

**28** **Look and write.**

dancer    singer    teacher    writer

1 _____    2 _____    3 _____    4 _____

**29** **Read and match.**

1 I want to protect animals.          a I want to be a nurse.
2 I want to help ill people.          b I want to be a lifeguard.
3 I want to grow food.               c I want to be a farmer.
4 I want to help people              d I want to be a park ranger.
  in the water.

**30** **Write.**

1 What does she want to be?

_____

2 What does he want to be?

_____

3 What do you want to be?

_____

**I Can**

☐ **talk about jobs.**
☐ **say what I want to be.**
☐ **talk about studying hard and setting goals.**

# My Day

2:38
**1** **Listen, look and say.**

**1:00** one o'clock

**2:00** two o'clock

**3:00** three o'clock

**4:00** four o'clock

**5:00** five o'clock

**6:00** six o'clock

**7:00** seven o'clock

**8:00** eight o'clock

**9:00** nine o'clock

**10:00** ten o'clock

**11:00** eleven o'clock

**12:00** twelve o'clock

2:39
**2** **Listen, find and say.**    **3** **Play a game.**

# 4  Listen and sing. Then look at 1 and find.

2:41 2:42

## What Time Is It?

Tick, tock. It's seven o'clock.
Time to get up and get dressed.
I want to stay in bed
But it's time to brush my teeth!

Tick, tock. It's eight o'clock.
At nine o'clock I start school.
I eat my breakfast and get my books.
I love school, it's cool!

Tick, tock. It's three o'clock.
There's no more school today.
I do my homework and I go out.
And there's my friend to play.

Now it's evening and it's eight o'clock
And it's time to go to bed.
I watch TV and read my book.
Time to sleep now, good night!

2:43

# 5  Look at 4. Listen and say yes or no.

# 6  Look at 1. Ask and answer.

What time is it?

It's one o'clock.

**THINK BIG**  What time is it now?
What time is it at midday?
What time is it at midnight?

2:45

**7** **Listen and read. When does Max get up?**

**8** **Look at the story. Number in order.**

☐ Max comes home.

☐ Max gets up.

☐ Max eats.

☐ Max sleeps again.

☐ Max goes out.

**THINK BIG** **What time do you go to bed?**
**What time do you get up?**
**How many hours do you sleep? Is that good or bad?**

2:46

**9 Listen. Help Jamie and Jenny make sentences.**

| go out | start school | watch TV | finish school |

| at 9:00 | at 7:00 | at 3:00 | at 12:00 |

When | does he get up | ?

He gets up | at 6:00 | .

When | do you go to bed | ?

I go to bed | at 8:00 | .

**10 Look and write do or does. Then answer the questions.**

**1** When _____ she eat lunch?
She _____
_____.

**2** When _____ they go to school?
They _____
_____.

**3** When _____ he brush his teeth?
He _____
_____.

2:48

**11 Listen and stick. Then say.**

**1**

**2**

**3**

**4**

**12 Look at 11. Ask and answer.**

When does she go to bed?

She goes to bed at ten o'clock.

**13 Look and write. Use start and finish.**

**1** When does the film start?
It starts at
_____.

**2** When does the film finish?
It finishes at
_____.

**3** When _____
school _____?

_____

_____

**4** _____

_____?

_____

_____

2:49

**14** Listen, repeat and find.

2:50

**15** Look, listen and read. Which clock uses sand to tell the time?

What time is it? How do you know? We use clocks, watches and mobile phones to tell the time. But there are other ways to tell the time. Some are very old.

**sundial**

**shadow**

**hourglass**

A **sundial** uses the sun to tell the time. The sun makes a shadow on the sundial. The shadow tells the time of day.

An **hourglass** uses sand to tell the time. Sand falls from the top of a glass to the bottom.

A **water clock** uses water to tell the time. It works like an hourglass. It's got two cups. The water falls from one cup to the other.

**water clock**

sand

**THINK BIG** Look, think and draw.

**16** **Circle T for true or F for false.**

1 We use clocks and watches to tell a story.    T    F

2 A sundial uses the sun to tell the time.    T    F

3 An hourglass uses water to tell the time.    T    F

4 A water clock works like an hourglass.    T    F

5 A water clock has got two cups.    T    F

**17** **Look and write.**

| clocks    hourglass    sand    sun    sundial    water clock |

1 We use _____ to tell the time.

2 A _____ uses water to tell the time.

3 A _____ uses the _____ to tell the time.

4 An _____ uses _____ to tell the time.

PROJECT

**18** **Make a Clock poster. Then present it to the class.**

Cuckoo! Cuckoo!

This is a cuckoo clock. It uses a cuckoo to tell the time. It's eleven o'clock.

2:51

 **Listen and number in order. Then say.**

a

I get dressed quickly
and eat breakfast.

b

I always get to school
on time.

c

I get my backpack ready
the night before school.

d

I get up early on
school days.

20 **Tell your partner how you get to school on time.
Do the actions.**

I get up early
on school days.

**THINK BIG** We all come to school at the same
time. Why is this good?
What other things is it good to be
on time for? Why?

2:52

 **21** **Listen, look and repeat.**

**1** ch          **2** tch          **3** sh

2:53

 **22** **Listen and find. Then say.**

**witch**          **ship**

**fish**          **chin**          **rich**

2:54

 **23** **Listen and blend the sounds.**

**1** ch-o-p    chop          **2** sh-o-p    shop

**3** m-a-tch  match          **4** l-u-n-ch  lunch

**5** d-i-sh      dish          **6** w-a-tch  watch

2:55

 **24** **Underline ch, tch and sh. Then listen and chant.**

Watch the witch,
She's having lunch!
Fish and chips
At the shop!

**25** **Play the Silly Sentences game.**

**First, write times on cards. Then write daily activities on other cards.**

**Now work in groups. Make two piles of cards. Take turns. Turn over one card from each pile and read a silly sentence.**

**26** **Look and write. What time is it?**

**1** It's _____.  **2** It's _____.  **3** It's _____.

**4** It's _____.  **5** It's _____.  **6** It's _____.

**27** **Circle. Then write the answers.**

**1** When **do** / **does** he get up?
He _____.

**2** When **do** / **does** you go to sleep?
I _____.

**28** **Find and write the words.**

**1** An _____ uses sand to tell the time. (galhossru)

**2** A _____ uses the sun to tell the time. (ladsuin)

**3** A water _____ uses water to tell the time. (ccolk)

**4** We use clocks and _____ to tell the time. (swtaech)

**I Can**
- ☐ talk about times and daily activities.
- ☐ say when people do things.
- ☐ talk about different ways of telling time.

**Do I Know It?**

1 **Think about it. Look and circle. Practise.**

😊 I know this. 😕 I don't know this.

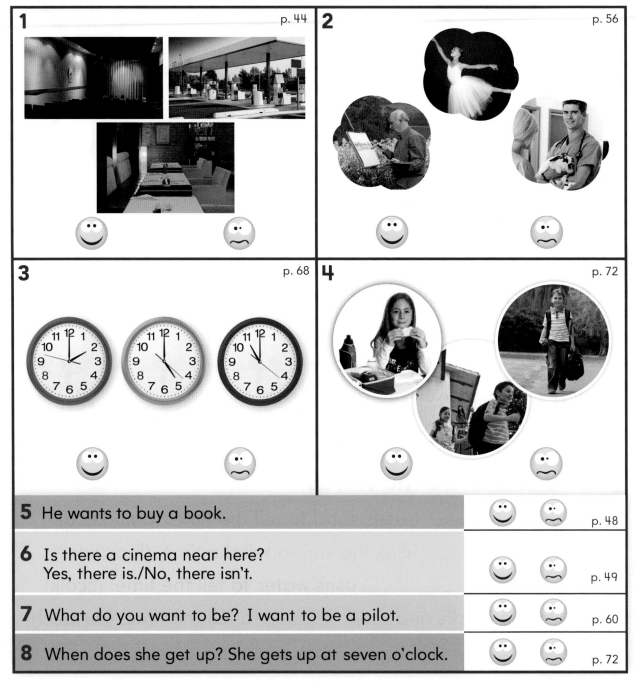

| | | |
|---|---|---|
| **5** He wants to buy a book. | 😊 😕 | p. 48 |
| **6** Is there a cinema near here? Yes, there is./No, there isn't. | 😊 😕 | p. 49 |
| **7** What do you want to be? I want to be a pilot. | 😊 😕 | p. 60 |
| **8** When does she get up? She gets up at seven o'clock. | 😊 😕 | p. 72 |

## I Can Do It!

2:57

**2** **Get ready.**

**A** Look, listen and write.

artist   athlete   teacher

**Charlie:** Hey, Linda, what do you want to be?

**Linda:** Well, I like running and I like jumping. I want to be an ¹_____.

**Charlie:** Really? What does your sister want to be?

**Linda:** She wants to be an ²_____.

**Charlie:** Why?

**Linda:** She likes drawing. She likes colouring pictures, too.

**Charlie:** I like Art, too.

**Linda:** Do you want to be an artist, Charlie?

**Charlie:** No, I don't. I want to be an Art ³_____. I like school!

**B** Talk about what you want to be. Say why.

What do you want to be?

I want to be a vet. I like animals.

**3** **Get set.**

STEP 1 Cut out the cards on page 141.

STEP 2 Put the cards on your desk. Mix the cards up.
Now you're ready to **Go!**

**4** **Go!**

**A** Take turns with a partner. Pick up a card. Continue until
you find a matching card. Read your cards aloud.

> I want to buy a book.

> Is there a bookshop
> near here?

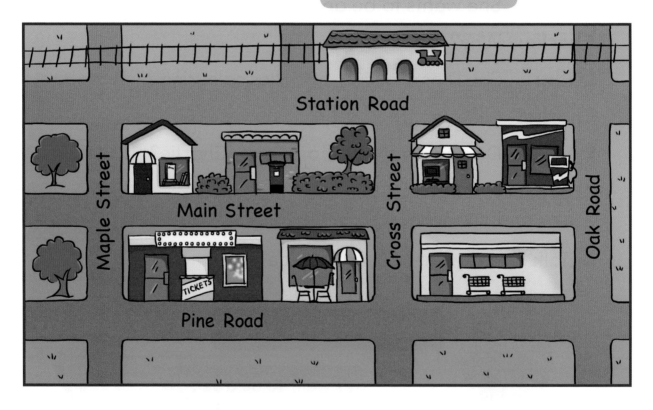

**B** Hold up one card at a time and find it on the map.
Ask and answer.

> Where's the bookshop?

> It's in Main Street.

**5** **Write or draw.**

 **All About Me**

| | |
|---|---|
| What do you want to be? | What time do you start school? |
| Where's your school? | When do you go to bed? |

**Do I Know It Now?**

**6** **Think about it.**

**A Go to page 80. Look and circle again.**

**B Tick (✔).**

☐ I can start the next unit.

☐ I can ask my teacher for help and then start the next unit.

☐ I can practise and then start the next unit.

**7** **Rate this Checkpoint. Colour the stars.**

 easy    hard         fun    not fun

1
2
3
4
5
6
7
8
9

# unit 7 My Favourite Food

 **1** Listen, look and say.

**1** bananas

**2** apples

**3** strawberries

**4** tomatoes

**5** carrots

**6** potatoes

**7** oranges

**8** mangoes

**9** cheese

**10** yoghurt

**11** vegetables

**12** sandwiches

**13** burgers

**14** snack

**15** meat

3:02

 **2** Listen, find and say.    **3** Play a game.

**84** Unit 7 vocabulary (food)

**4** **Listen and sing. Then look at 1 and find.**

## Let's Eat Lunch!

It's twelve o'clock.
Let's eat lunch.
Do you like bananas?
I like them for lunch!

Do you like tomatoes?
Yes, I do. I like tomatoes. I really do.
Do you like potatoes?
Yes, I do. I like potatoes, too. Do you?

Meat and fruit,
Vegetables and snacks,
I like them all.
Can I have more, please?

Have some chips
And a burger, too.
Let's share some ice cream.
I like eating lunch with you!

 **5** **Listen, match and write.**

I like _____. I like _____. I like _____.

 **1**    **2**    **3**

**a**    **b**    **c**

**6** **Look at 1. Ask and answer.**

Do you like bananas?

Yes, I do. I like bananas.

 **THINK BIG** **Which pictures show fruit?**
**Which pictures show vegetables?**

3:07

**7** **Listen and read. Does Dan like apples?**

Do You Like Fruit?

It's four o'clock, boys. Do you want a snack?

Yes, please, Dad.

1

There's fruit. Does Dan like fruit?

Yes, he does.

2

But I don't like bananas.

Jamie doesn't like bananas, either.

3

Do you like mangoes?

Yes, I do. I like mangoes.

4

**8** **Look at the story. Write yes or no.**

**1** Does Dan like fruit? _____

**2** Does Jamie like bananas? _____

**3** Does Dan like mangoes? _____

**4** Do the boys like pie? _____

**5** Is it a banana pie? _____

THINK BIG **What fruit do you like?**
**What dishes can you make with fruit?**

**9** Listen. Help Jamie and Jenny make sentences.

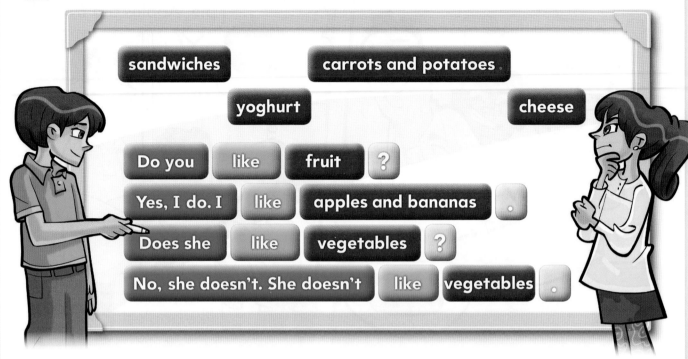

sandwiches          carrots and potatoes

yoghurt                                    cheese

Do you | like | fruit | ?

Yes, I do. I | like | apples and bananas | .

Does she | like | vegetables | ?

No, she doesn't. She doesn't | like | vegetables | .

**10** Look and write. Then answer.

**1** _____ she like strawberries?
Yes, she _____. She _____ strawberries.

**2** _____ he like tomatoes?
No, he _____. He _____ tomatoes.

**3** _____ they like sandwiches?
Yes, they _____. They _____ sandwiches.

**4** Do _____ like oranges?
_____, I _____. I _____ oranges.

3:10

 **11** **Listen and stick. Then say.**

**1**

**2**

**3**

**4**

**12** **Look at 11. Ask and answer.**

Do you like strawberries?

No, I don't. I like apples.

**13** **Draw and write. Do you like vegetables?**

_____

_____

_____

3:11
**14** **Listen, repeat and find.**

 3:12
**15** **Look, listen and read. Which fruit comes from China?**

# Where Fruit Comes From

Some snacks, like chocolate, are unhealthy. Others, like fruit, are very healthy. But where does fruit come from?

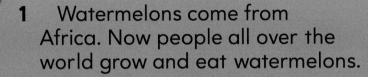

**1** Watermelons come from Africa. Now people all over the world grow and eat watermelons.

**watermelon**

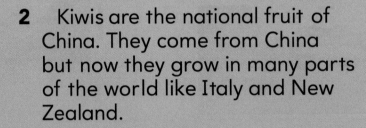

**2** Kiwis are the national fruit of China. They come from China but now they grow in many parts of the world like Italy and New Zealand.

**kiwi**

**pineapple**

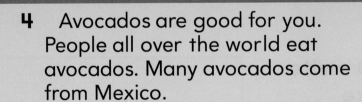

**3** People from many parts of the world like pineapples. They come from South America but now they grow in many parts of the world where it is warm.

**4** Avocados are good for you. People all over the world eat avocados. Many avocados come from Mexico.

**avocado**

**THINK BIG** Fruit is a healthy snack. Can you think of other healthy snacks?
Chocolate is an unhealthy snack. Can you think of other unhealthy snacks?

**16** Read again. Write the names of the fruit under the places they come from.

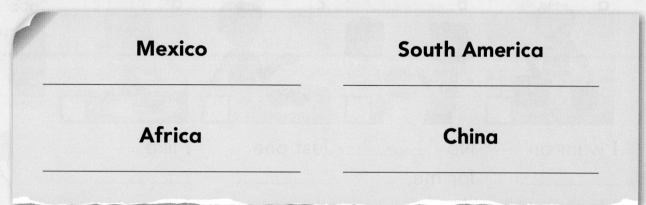

| Mexico | South America |
|---|---|
| _____ | _____ |
| Africa | China |
| _____ | _____ |

3:13

**17** Listen and say true or false. Then play a game.

Pineapples come from Africa.

False.

**18** Make a Where Fruit Comes From poster. Then present it to the class.

Where fruit comes from

Tomatoes come from South America. Bananas come from Africa.

3:14

**19** **Listen and number. Then write and say.**

| a | b | c | d |
|---|---|---|---|
|  |  |  |  |

apple
biscuit
carrots
crisps

I want an _____, please.

No _____ for me, thanks.

Just one _____, please.

I like _____.

**20** **Look and circle. Then look at 19 and role play.**

**1**

healthy / unhealthy

**2**

healthy / unhealthy

**3**

healthy / unhealthy

**4**

healthy / unhealthy

**5**

healthy / unhealthy

**6**

healthy / unhealthy

I want a carrot, please.

No chocolate for me, thanks.

**THINK BIG** **What healthy food did you eat today?**
**What unhealthy food did you eat today?**

**3:15**

**21 Listen, look and repeat.**

**1** ee          **2** ie

 **3:16**

**22 Listen and find. Then say.**

**sheep**

**pie**

**bee**

**tie**

 **3:17**

**23 Listen and blend the sounds.**

**1** f-ee-t     feet          **2** l-ie        lie

**3** s-ee        see          **4** f-l-ie-s   flies

**5** ch-ee-se cheese        **6** c-r-ie-d   cried

**3:18**

**24 Underline ee and ie. Then listen and chant.**

"See the cheese!"
Cried the bees.
"See the pies!"
Cried the flies.

# Review

**25** **Play the What Do You Like? game.**

**1** Circle yes for the foods you like. Circle no for the foods you don't like.

**2** Guess what your partner likes. Circle.

**3** Your partner says what he or she likes. Tick (✓) your correct guesses.

|  | YOU | | YOUR PARTNER | | CORRECT? |
|---|---|---|---|---|---|
| **1 carrots** | yes | no | yes | no | |
| **2 cheese** | yes | no | yes | no | |
| **3 tomatoes** | yes | no | yes | no | |
| **4 mangoes** | yes | no | yes | no | |
| **5 oranges** | yes | no | yes | no | |
| **6 burgers** | yes | no | yes | no | |
| **7 sandwiches** | yes | no | yes | no | |
| **8 meat** | yes | no | yes | no | |
| **9 strawberries** | yes | no | yes | no | |
| **10 potatoes** | yes | no | yes | no | |

Greg, do you like carrots?

Yes, I do.

Greg likes carrots. He doesn't like cheese.

**26** **Tell the class what your partner likes and doesn't like.**

**27 Look and write. Use likes/doesn't like or like/don't like.**

1 She _____ biscuits.

2 They _____ sandwiches.

3 They _____ cheese.

4 He _____ vegetables.

5 He _____ carrots.

6 She _____ bananas.

**28 Find and write the words.**

1 _____ come from Africa. (meWtalnosre)

2 _____ come from Mexico. (sadvoAco)

3 _____ come from China. (wiiKs)

4 _____ come from South America. (sipplPneae)

**I Can**

☐ talk about food I like.
☐ talk about healthy and unhealthy food.
☐ say where fruit comes from.

# unit 8

# Wild Animals

**1** Listen, look and say.

1 giraffe

2 hippo

3 kangaroo

4 cheetah

5 polar bear

6 zebra

7 parrot

8 monkey

9 peacock

10 elephant

11 crocodile

12 snake

3:21

**2** Listen, find and say.    **3** Play a game.

## 4 Listen and sing. Then look at 1 and find.

### To the Zoo!

I really like animals!
Do you like them, too?
That's why I'm so happy.
We're going to the zoo!

A kangaroo can jump.
A monkey can jump, too.
Crocodiles can chase
And swim.
And you, what can you do?

A giraffe can't fly or jump up high.
An elephant can't climb trees.
Fish can't run and hippos can't fly.
Come and see them.
Oh, yes, please!

Now it's time to say goodbye
To every animal here.
But we can come back
And see them every year!

## 5 Listen and say true or false.

## 6 Look at 1. Ask and answer.

Do you like cheetahs?

Yes, I do! Cheetahs can run.

**THINK BIG** Which animals can chase other animals? Which animals can climb trees?

3:26

**(7) Listen and read. What animals does Jamie like?**

**Monkeys Are Great!**

What's your favourite animal?

I like monkeys best.

**1**

Why do you like monkeys?

Monkeys are great! They can climb trees. They can jump.

**2**

Well, I like hippos.

**3**

Hippos? Can a hippo jump?

No, it can't.

**4**

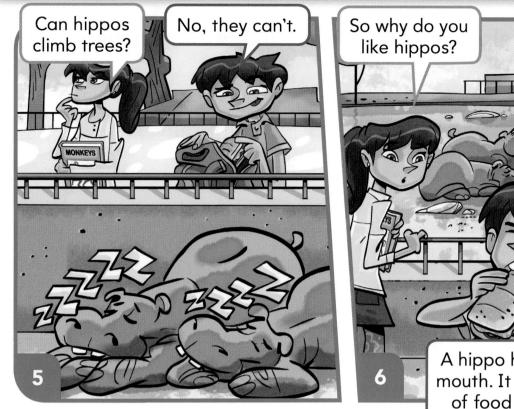

**8** **Look. Circle can or can't.**

1 Monkeys **can / can't** climb trees.
2 Monkeys **can / can't** jump.
3 Hippos **can / can't** climb trees.
4 Hippos **can / can't** jump.
5 Hippos **can / can't** eat a lot.
6 Jamie **can / can't** eat a lot.

**THINK BIG** **What animals can swim, run and eat fish?**
**What animals can't fly or climb trees?**

**9** Listen. Help Jamie and Jenny make sentences.

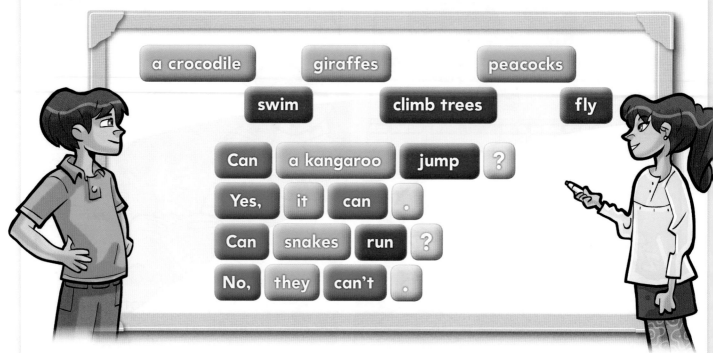

a crocodile    giraffes    peacocks

swim    climb trees    fly

Can | a kangaroo | jump | ?

Yes, | it | can | .

Can | snakes | run | ?

No, | they | can't | .

**10** Look and write. Then draw and write.

**1** _____ a zebra see at night?

Yes, _____.

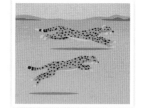

**2** _____ cheetahs run?

Yes, _____.

**3** _____ a giraffe climb trees?

No, _____.

**4** _____

_____

3:28

**11 Listen and stick. Then write.**

elephants   kangaroos   monkeys   snakes

**1** Can _____ climb trees?

**2** Can _____ run?

**3** Can _____ play?

**4** Can _____ fly?

**12 Look at 11. Ask and answer.**

Can monkeys climb trees?

Yes, they can.

**13 Write and draw. Then say.**

_____

_____

_____

**3:29**

**14** Listen, repeat and find.

**3:30**

**15** Look, listen and read. Where do monkeys live?

# Animal Habitats

Animals need food, water, air and a place to live.
A habitat is the place where an animal lives.

### forest

**1** The forest is a cool, dark place with lots of trees. Deer, raccoons and foxes live in forests.

### desert

**2** The desert is hot and dry during the day and cold at night. There are not many trees or plants there. Lizards and snakes live in deserts.

### ocean

**3** Some animals live in the water. The biggest body of water is called an ocean. Many kinds of fish live in oceans. Other animals live there, too, like whales, sharks and seals.

### jungle

**4** The jungle is hot and wet. It rains a lot. There are lots of trees in the jungle. Monkeys and colourful birds live in jungles. There are some very big cats, too!

**THINK BIG** What habitats are there in your country? Are there jungles, forests, deserts or oceans? What animals live in them?

**16** Write the habitats. Then match each animal to its habitat.

**1** _____

**2** _____

**3** _____

**a**

snake

**b**

fox

**c**

whale

**17** Look at 16. Ask and answer.

Can they swim?  Yes.

Do they live in oceans?  Yes.

Are they whales?  Yes.

## PROJECT

**18** Make an Animal Habitats poster. Then present it to the class.

Tigers live in jungles.

3:31

**19 Listen and number. Then say.**

a

b

c

d

I think peacocks are beautiful.

Monkeys are so clever.

Giraffes are amazing. Their necks are so long.

Elephants are very strong.

**20 Look at 19. Ask and answer.**

| amazing | beautiful | clever | strong |

What animal do you like?

I like parrots. They're so beautiful.

THINK BIG **What is your favourite animal? Why?**

3:33

**21** **Listen, look and repeat.**

**1** OU        **2** OW

3:34

**22** **Listen and find. Then say.**

cow

soup

owl

You

you

3:35

**23** **Listen and blend the sounds.**

**1** g-r-ou-p        group          **2** t-ow-n          town

**3** t-ou-c-a-n      toucan         **4** c-l-ow-n        clown

**5** d-ow-n          down           **6** r-ou-te         route

3:36

**24** **Underline ou and ow. Then listen and chant.**

An owl went
Down to town
To see a group
Of toucans
Drinking soup.

## 25 Play the What Animal Am I? game.

**Step 1.** Write the name of an animal on a sticky note. Don't show your partner.

**Step 2.** Stick your note on your partner's forehead. Your partner asks you questions and guesses the animal.

**Step 3.** Now play with other partners.

**26** **Look and write.**

**1** Can _____ swim?

No, _____ .

**2** Can a _____ fly?

No, _____ .

**3** Can _____ run?

_____

**4** Can a _____ jump?

_____

**27** **Read and circle.**

**1** Whales live in **jungles** / **oceans**.

**2** Monkeys live in **jungles** / **deserts**.

**3** Fish live in **forests** / **oceans**.

**4** Foxes live in **jungles** / **forests**.

**I Can**

☐ **talk about what animals can do.**

☐ **talk about where animals live.**

☐ **talk about appreciating animals.**

# unit 9 Fun All Year

3:38

**1** Listen, look and say.

## January
| SUN | MON | TUE | WED | THU | FRI | SAT |
| --- | --- | --- | --- | --- | --- | --- |
| 1 | 2 | 3 | 4 | 5 | 6 | 7 |
| 8 | 9 | 10 | 11 | 12 | 13 | 14 |
| 15 | 16 | 17 | 18 | 19 | 20 | 21 |
| 22 | 23 | 24 | 25 | 26 | 27 | 28 |
| 29 | 30 | 31 | | | | |

## February
| SUN | MON | TUE | WED | THU | FRI | SAT |
| --- | --- | --- | --- | --- | --- | --- |
| | | | 1 | 2 | 3 | 4 |
| 5 | 6 | 7 | 8 | 9 | 10 | 11 |
| 12 | 13 | 14 | 15 | 16 | 17 | 18 |
| 19 | 20 | 21 | 22 | 23 | 24 | 25 |
| 26 | 27 | 28 | 29 | | | |

## March
| SUN | MON | TUE | WED | THU | FRI | SAT |
| --- | --- | --- | --- | --- | --- | --- |
| | | | | 1 | 2 | 3 |
| 4 | 5 | 6 | 7 | 8 | 9 | 10 |
| 11 | 12 | 13 | 14 | 15 | 16 | 17 |
| 18 | 19 | 20 | 21 | 22 | 23 | 24 |
| 25 | 26 | 27 | 28 | 29 | 30 | 31 |

## April
| SUN | MON | TUE | WED | THU | FRI | SAT |
| --- | --- | --- | --- | --- | --- | --- |
| 1 | 2 | 3 | 4 | 5 | 6 | 7 |
| 8 | 9 | 10 | 11 | 12 | 13 | 14 |
| 15 | 16 | 17 | 18 | 19 | 20 | 21 |
| 22 | 23 | 24 | 25 | 26 | 27 | 28 |
| 29 | 30 | | | | | |

## May
| SUN | MON | TUE | WED | THU | FRI | SAT |
| --- | --- | --- | --- | --- | --- | --- |
| | | 1 | 2 | 3 | 4 | 5 |
| 6 | 7 | 8 | 9 | 10 | 11 | 12 |
| 13 | 14 | 15 | 16 | 17 | 18 | 19 |
| 20 | 21 | 22 | 23 | 24 | 25 | 26 |
| 27 | 28 | 29 | 30 | 31 | | |

## June
| SUN | MON | TUE | WED | THU | FRI | SAT |
| --- | --- | --- | --- | --- | --- | --- |
| | | | | | 1 | 2 |
| 3 | 4 | 5 | 6 | 7 | 8 | 9 |
| 10 | 11 | 12 | 13 | 14 | 15 | 16 |
| 17 | 18 | 19 | 20 | 21 | 22 | 23 |
| 24 | 25 | 26 | 27 | 28 | 29 | 30 |

## July
| SUN | MON | TUE | WED | THU | FRI | SAT |
| --- | --- | --- | --- | --- | --- | --- |
| 1 | 2 | 3 | 4 | 5 | 6 | 7 |
| 8 | 9 | 10 | 11 | 12 | 13 | 14 |
| 15 | 16 | 17 | 18 | 19 | 20 | 21 |
| 22 | 23 | 24 | 25 | 26 | 27 | 28 |
| 29 | 30 | 31 | | | | |

## August
| SUN | MON | TUE | WED | THU | FRI | SAT |
| --- | --- | --- | --- | --- | --- | --- |
| | | | 1 | 2 | 3 | 4 |
| 5 | 6 | 7 | 8 | 9 | 10 | 11 |
| 12 | 13 | 14 | 15 | 16 | 17 | 18 |
| 19 | 20 | 21 | 22 | 23 | 24 | 25 |
| 26 | 27 | 28 | 29 | 30 | 31 | |

## September
| SUN | MON | TUE | WED | THU | FRI | SAT |
| --- | --- | --- | --- | --- | --- | --- |
| | | | | | | 1 |
| 2 | 3 | 4 | 5 | 6 | 7 | 8 |
| 9 | 10 | 11 | 12 | 13 | 14 | 15 |
| 16 | 17 | 18 | 19 | 20 | 21 | 22 |
| 23 | 24 | 25 | 26 | 27 | 28 | 29 |
| 30 | | | | | | |

## October
| SUN | MON | TUE | WED | THU | FRI | SAT |
| --- | --- | --- | --- | --- | --- | --- |
| | 1 | 2 | 3 | 4 | 5 | 6 |
| 7 | 8 | 9 | 10 | 11 | 12 | 13 |
| 14 | 15 | 16 | 17 | 18 | 19 | 20 |
| 21 | 22 | 23 | 24 | 25 | 26 | 27 |
| 28 | 29 | 30 | 31 | | | |

## November
| SUN | MON | TUE | WED | THU | FRI | SAT |
| --- | --- | --- | --- | --- | --- | --- |
| | | | | 1 | 2 | 3 |
| 4 | 5 | 6 | 7 | 8 | 9 | 10 |
| 11 | 12 | 13 | 14 | 15 | 16 | 17 |
| 18 | 19 | 20 | 21 | 22 | 23 | 24 |
| 25 | 26 | 27 | 28 | 29 | 30 | |

## December
| SUN | MON | TUE | WED | THU | FRI | SAT |
| --- | --- | --- | --- | --- | --- | --- |
| | | | | | | 1 |
| 2 | 3 | 4 | 5 | 6 | 7 | 8 |
| 9 | 10 | 11 | 12 | 13 | 14 | 15 |
| 16 | 17 | 18 | 19 | 20 | 21 | 22 |
| 23 | 24 | 25 | 26 | 27 | 28 | 29 |
| 30 | 31 | | | | | |

3:39

**2**  Listen, find and say.   **3** Play a game.

**108** Unit 9 vocabulary (months of the year)

**4** **Listen and chant. Then look at 1 and find.**

### I Like July!

July is my favourite month.
I like August, too.
I'm happy and on holiday,
There is so much to do!

I also like September.
That's when I start school.
I'm so excited, aren't you?
My friends will be there, too!

I don't like December.
It is so very cold.
But then it is my birthday, too.
This year I'm eight years old!

3:42

**5** **Listen and write the month.**

1 _____   2 _____   3 _____

**6** **Look at 1. Ask and answer.**

What's your favourite month?

I like May.

**THINK BIG** Which months are holiday months at school?

3:44

**7** Listen and read. When is Jamie's birthday?

## Fun in August!

What's your favourite month, Jenny?

I like December. We always go on holiday in December.

**1**

Do you go on holiday in winter?

No, I never go on holiday in winter. It's too cold!

**2**

I always go on holiday in August. I love swimming in the sea.

**3**

What do you do in August, Jamie?

I always have fun in August. It's my birthday!

**4**

**5** I never go to school. I always have a big party!

**6** And Mum always makes a big chocolate cake! August is my favourite month!

**8** Look at the story. Circle.

1 Jenny's favourite month is **January** / **December**.
2 Dan goes swimming in **January** / **August**.
3 Jamie's favourite month is **August** / **May**.
4 Jenny always goes on holiday in **December** / **November**.
5 Dan never goes on holiday in **August** / **December**.
6 Jamie always has a party in **April** / **August**.

**THINK BIG** When do you go on holiday?
I always go on holiday in _____.
I never go on holiday in _____.

3:45

**9** Listen. Help Jamie and Jenny make sentences.

| in April | in June | in summer |

play in the park | go to school | swim in the sea

What does he | do | in January | ?

He always | has a New Year's party | in January | .

Do you | go on holiday | in May | ?

No, I don't. I never | go on holiday | in May | .

**10** Write and circle.

**1** What does she do in summer? Does she play tennis?
Yes, she _____. She **always** / **never** plays tennis
in summer.

**2** What _____ you do in February? Do you go
on holiday?
No, we _____. We **always** / **never** go on holiday
in February.

**3** Do they go to school in September?
Yes, they _____. They **always** / **never** go to
school in September.

**4** Do you go to the park in winter?
_____. I **always** / **never** go to the
park in winter.

3:46

 **11** **Listen and stick. Then write the number.**

**a**

We always swim in the sea.

**b**

We always go to my grandad's house.

**c**

We always go on holiday.

**d**

I always play football with my friends.

**12** **Look at 11. Ask and answer.**

Do you go on holiday in April?

No, I don't. I never go on holiday in April.

**13** **Write and draw. What do you do in winter?**

I _____

_____

in winter.

3:47

**14** Look, listen and repeat.

**1 winter**        **2 spring**        **3 summer**        **4 autumn**

3:48

**15** Look, listen and read. Which festival is in spring?

# Celebrating Special Days

**1**    In China, people celebrate the **mid-Autumn** festival. This festival happens in September or October when the moon is very big and bright. Children wear colourful masks and dance in the streets. They also eat sweet mooncakes.

**2**    Children in England celebrate spring on the 1st May. On **May Day**, people put flowers and ribbons on a pole. Children dance around this maypole to welcome spring.

**3**    In Japan, people celebrate the star festival, **Tanabata**, in summer. On the 7th July, people write wishes on small pieces of paper. They hang the wishes on bamboo to make a 'wish tree'.

**4**    In winter, people all over the world celebrate **New Year's Eve**. This festival comes on the last day of the year, the 31st December. People go to parties and watch fireworks.

**THINK BIG** What festivals do people celebrate in your country?

**16** **Look at 15. Choose and write.**

| autumn | spring | summer | winter |

**1** People in China celebrate the mid-_____ festival.

**2** Children in England celebrate May Day to welcome _____.

**3** In Japan, people celebrate Tanabata in _____.

**4** People celebrate New Year's Eve in _____.

**17** **Look and say. Then ask your friends.**

| Name | Favourite Festival | When? |
|------|--------------------|-------|
|      |                    |       |
|      |                    |       |
|      |                    |       |

What's your favourite festival?

My favourite festival is Carnival.

When do you celebrate Carnival?

We celebrate Carnival in spring.

**PROJECT**

**18** **Make a Festival poster. Then present it to the class.**

Winter

People celebrate New Year's Eve in winter.

In my country, people celebrate New Year's Eve in winter.

3:50

 **19** **Listen and write the season. Then say.**

autumn    spring    winter    summer

**1**

**2**

**3**

**4**

In _____, they skate on ice.

In _____, he rides his bike.

In _____, she likes to swim.

In _____, they rake leaves.

**20** **Draw and write. What do you do in each season?**

**1** In summer, _____
_____.

**2** In winter, _____
_____.

**21** **Look at 20. Ask and answer.**

What do you do in winter?

In winter, I do gymnastics.

**THINK BIG** **What can you only do in winter? Why?**
**What can you only do in summer? Why?**

**3:51**
**22** **Listen, look and say.**

| Aa | Bb | Cc | Dd | Ee | |
|----|----|----|----|----|---|
| Ff | Gg | Hh | Ii | Jj | |
| Kk | Ll | Mm | Nn | Oo | |
| Pp | Qq | Rr | Ss | Tt | |
| Uu | Vv | Ww | Xx | Yy | Zz |

**3:52**
**23** **Listen, look and chant. Can you find something starting with every letter of the alphabet?**

A, B, C, D, E, F, G.
I can see an ant and a bat. What can you see?
H, I, J, K, L, M, N, O, P.
I can see a hat and some ink. What can you see?
Q, R, S, T, U, V.
I can see a rat and a snake. What can you see?
W, X, Y and Z.
I can see six yellow wolves and a zebra, I said!

**24  Play the Months Line-Up game.**

**Step 1.** Ask when your classmates' birthdays are. Then line up in order by month.

> When is your birthday?

> It's in November. When's yours?

> My birthday is in July.

**Step 2.** Check the order with the class.

> My birthday is in January.

> My birthday is in August.

> My birthday is in November.

**Step 3.** Play the game again. Ask and answer. Then line up again by month.

1  What is your favourite month?

2  What is your favourite holiday?

3  When is your favourite school event?

**25** **Number the months in order.**

July ☐

May ☐

October ☐

February ☐

September ☐

January ☐

November ☐

June ☐

April ☐

December ☐

March ☐

August ☐

**26** **Write about you.**

**1** What do you do in winter?

I always _____ in winter.

I never _____ in winter.

**2** What do you do in summer?

I always _____ in summer.

I never _____ in summer.

**3** What do you do in autumn?

I always _____ in autumn.

I never _____ in autumn.

**4** What do you do in spring?

I always _____ in spring.

I never _____ in spring.

**I Can**

☐ **name the months of the year.**

☐ **talk about what I do each month.**

☐ **talk about seasonal holidays.**

**Do I Know It?**

**1** **Think about it. Look and circle. Practise.**

😊 I know this.  😟 I don't know this.

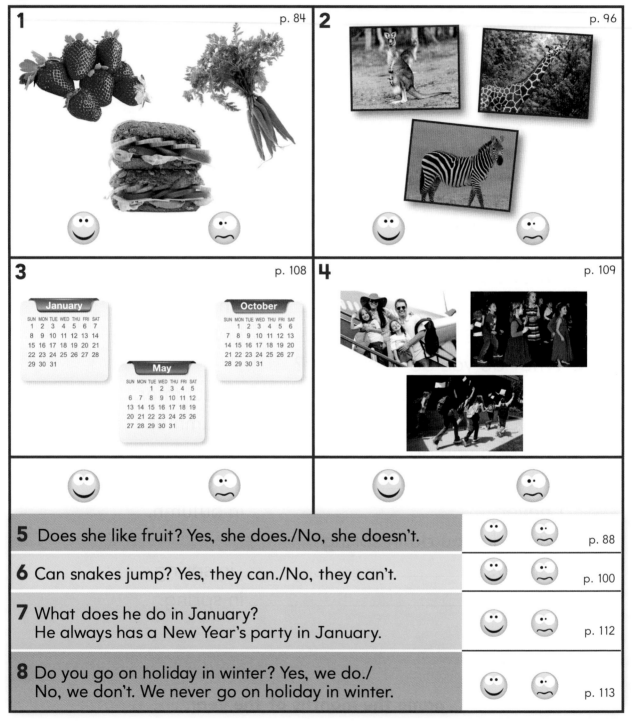

| | |
|---|---|
| **5** Does she like fruit? Yes, she does./No, she doesn't. | 😊 😟 p. 88 |
| **6** Can snakes jump? Yes, they can./No, they can't. | 😊 😟 p. 100 |
| **7** What does he do in January? <br> He always has a New Year's party in January. | 😊 😟 p. 112 |
| **8** Do you go on holiday in winter? Yes, we do./ <br> No, we don't. We never go on holiday in winter. | 😊 😟 p. 113 |

**I Can Do It!**

3:55

**2 Get ready.**

**A** Look, listen and write.

> always   can   can't   never

**Alan:**    Is that your parrot? He's so beautiful!

**Tess:**    Yes. His name is Crackers. He's very clever.
He ¹_____ talk!

**Alan:**    He can?

**Tess:**    Yes, he can.

**Alan:**    That's amazing! Does he like fruit?

**Tess:**    Yes, he does. He likes bananas,
mangoes and apples.

**Alan:**    Oh!

**Tess:**    He can sing, too.

**Alan:**    Really?

**Tess:**    Yes. He ²_____ sings to
me in the morning!

**Alan:**    Wow. My cat is so boring. She ³_____
say anything and she ⁴_____ sings
to me!

**B** Look at A. Ask and answer.

> What can Crackers do?

> What can't Alan's cat do?

> Does Crackers like fruit?

**3** **Get set.**

✂ **STEP 1** Cut out the outline on page 143. Cut each card in half along the dotted line.

📒 **STEP 2** Sort the cards into two piles. Put the heads of the animals in one pile and the bodies in the other. Now you're ready to **Go!**

**4** **Go!**

**A** Put one card from each of your piles together to make a funny animal.

**B** Talk about your funny animals. Ask and answer.

This is an elebra!

Can elebras climb trees?

No, they can't.

Do they like fruit?

Yes, they do. They like oranges and mangoes.

**C** Look at others' animals. Who's got the same animal as you?

**5** Write or draw.

# All About Me

| | |
|---|---|
| When is your birthday? | What do you like eating for lunch? |
| What's your favourite month? | What do you always do in summer? |

**Do I Know It Now?**

**6** Think about it.

**A** Go to page 120. Look and circle again.

**B** Tick (✔).

☐ I can ask my teacher for help.

☐ I can practise.

**7** Rate this Checkpoint. Colour the stars.

easy    hard

fun    not fun

# Young Learners English Practice Starters: Listening A

## – 5 questions –

 **Look at the pictures. Now listen and look. There is one example.**

What's Alex doing?

A ☐

B ☑

C ☐

**1** What's Jill doing?

A ☐

B ☐

C ☐

**2** What's Ben doing?

A ☐

B ☐

C ☐

**3** Where's Pat's jacket?

**A** ☐

**B** ☐

**C** ☐

**4** How many people are in the picture?

**A** ☐

**B** ☐

**C** ☐

**5** What are Bill and Ann doing?

**A** ☐

**B** ☐

**C** ☐

– 5 questions –

**Look at the picture. Listen and write a name or a number. There are two examples.**

**Examples**

| What is the boy's name? | *Tom* |
|---|---|
| How old is he? | *10* |

## Questions

**1** How old is Sara? _____

**2** How many books has Tom got? _____

**3** What's the cat's name? _____

**4** What's the dog's name? _____

**5** Where's the library? in _____ Street

# Young Learners English Practice Starters: Listening C

## – 5 questions –

 **Look at the pictures. Now listen and look. There is one example.**

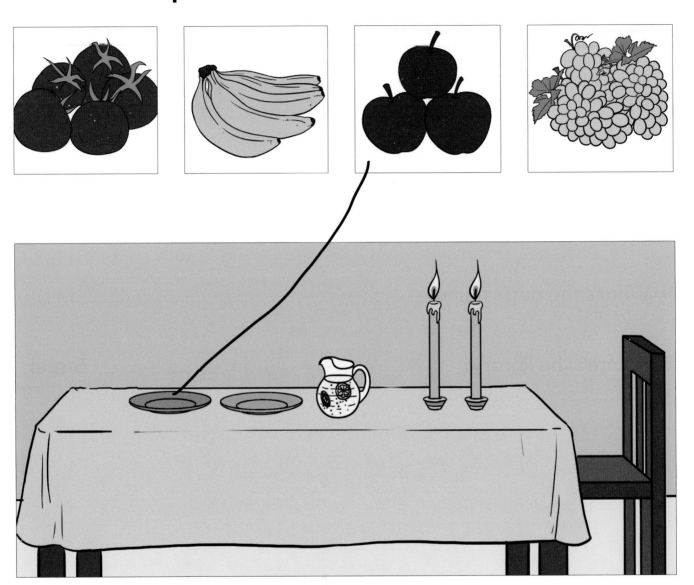

# Young Learners English Practice Starters: Reading & Writing A

## – 5 questions –

**Look at the pictures. Look at the letters. Write the words.**

**Example**

<u>s w i n g</u>          g w i n s

**Questions**

1

_ _ _ _ _ _ _ _          r e t m o c u p

2

_ _ _ _ _          d e s l i

3

_ _ _ _ _ _ _ _ _          t a s k e d r a b o

4

_ _ _ _ _ _          n e c l i p

5

_ _ _ _ _ _ _          r e t i c u p

## – 5 questions –

**Look and read. Put a tick (✓) or an (X) in the box.
There are two examples.**

## Examples

She is a doctor. ✔

This is a bus stop. ✗

## Questions

1

This is a bookshop. ☐

**2**

She is a dancer. ☐

**3**

He is a teacher. ☐

**4**

This is a petrol station. ☐

**5**

He is a singer. ☐

**– 5 questions –**

**Read. Choose a word from the box. Write the correct word next to numbers 1–5. There is one example.**

## A Zoo

I am a big place. A lot of animals live in me. The _elephant_ has got big ears and a long trunk. The ¹_____ is a bird with a beautiful tail. The ²_____ is another beautiful bird. It likes talking. Then there are ³_____. They've got long tails and live in my trees. The ⁴_____ is a large, grey animal with small ears. It likes the water. And the ⁵_____ has got a long neck and spots. What am I? I am a zoo.

| example | | | |
|---|---|---|---|
| elephant | peacock | giraffe | hippo |
| kangaroo | monkeys | toucan | snake |

# Young Learners English Practice Starters: Speaking

# Wordlist

# Wordlist

# Big English Song

From the mountaintops to the bottom of the sea,
From a big blue whale to a baby bumblebee-
If you're big, if you're small, you can have it all
And you can be anything you want to be!

**It's bigger than you. It's bigger than me.
There's so much to do and there's so much to see!
The world is big and beautiful and so are we!
Think big! Dream big! Big English!**

So in every land, from the desert to the sea
We can all join hands and be one big family.
If we love, if we care, we can go anywhere!
The world belongs to everyone; it's ours to share.

**It's bigger than you. It's bigger than me.
There's so much to do and there's so much to see!
The world is big and beautiful and so are we!
Think big! Dream big! Big English!**

**It's bigger than you. It's bigger than me.
There's so much to do and there's so much to see!
The world is big and beautiful and waiting for me.
A One, two, three...
Think big! Dream big! Big English!**

| | |
|---|---|
| We want to go to the post office. | Is there a post office near here? |
| I want to buy a book. | Is there a bookshop near here? |
| My mum wants to eat lunch. | Is there a restaurant near here? |
| My grandma wants to buy biscuits and milk. | Is there a supermarket near here? |
| My dad wants to put petrol in the car. | Is there a petrol station near here? |